Magic Managed

"Finding the magic in the middle of the struggle"

K. A. Bauer

Published by Hemingway Publishers

Cover design by Hemingway Publishers

ISBN: Printed in the United States

TABLE OF CONTENTS

SUNRISE, SUNRISE

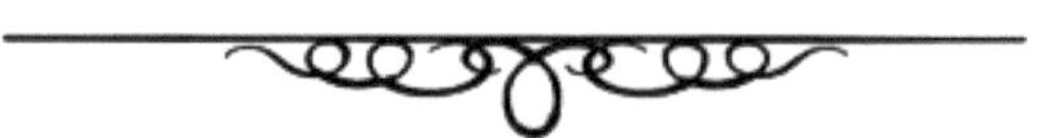

The sky begins in hushed and shadowed grey,
A silent stage before the birth of the day,
Until a ribbon, thin and pale as bone,
Across the far horizon, a sound starts to moan.

Then comes the lemon, soft and shyly bright,
The first low whisper of the coming light.
It spills to apricot, a warmth that grows,
Transforming clouds to petals of a rose;

A wash of lavender and bruised plum hues,
That drift and linger in the morning dews,
Where violet shadows lose their cooling grip,
As amber honey starts to slowly drip.

Then sudden crimson breaks the eastern line,
A rush of ruby, potent and divine,
Staining the heavens in a burning fan,
A fire that started since the world began.

The gold ascends, a crown of molten heat,
To lay its shimmering carpet at your feet.

The blue returns, a clear and crystal bowl,
The vibrant colors resting in the soul,
Until the day is fully, brightly born,
In all the painted glory of the morn.

THE KNIGHT OF THE NURSERY

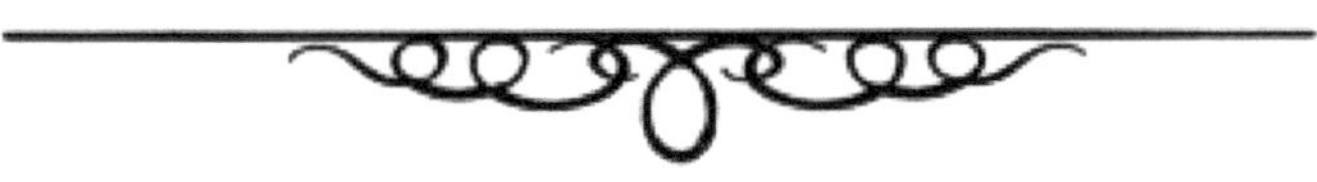

By the light of the sun, he is soft, plush, and still,
With a velvet-eared grin and a heart of goodwill.
He sits at the table for crumpets and tea,
The gentlest companion that a person could be.

He listens to stories, he shares in the play,
A fuzzy pawed shadow through the heat of the day.
But when the clock strikes a late, lonely hour,
The stuffing turns steel, and the fabric turns power.

For when the moon rises, and the hallways grow long,
The Bear becomes heavy, and the Bear becomes strong.
With two silver swords strapped tight to his back,
And a gun on his hip for the midnight attack.

He steps from the shelf as the city goes dim,
For the safety of the realm rests on him.
Upon the dark road, where the shadows are deep,
The Wanderer marches while the innocent sleep.

He fears no darkness, no monster, no ghost,
He stands at the border, a one-man strong host.
A Warrior Lark in the silver blue light,
He hunts back the cold, and he conquers the night.

With a blade in his hand and a flint in his eye,
He's the master of stars in the vast, velvet sky.
A protector of realms, a silent, brave guard,
Patrolling the hallways and the moon-dusted yard.

Then, just as the dawn starts to break in the east,
The Soldier retreats, and the battle has ceased.
He holsters his weapons, he smooths down his fur,
Until not a trace of the hero can stir.

He's back in his chair as the morning grows bright,
Ready for tea and the soft, golden light.
No one's the wiser for the blood and the grit
Just a Bear and his tea, and the magic of it.

THE GEOMETRY OF US

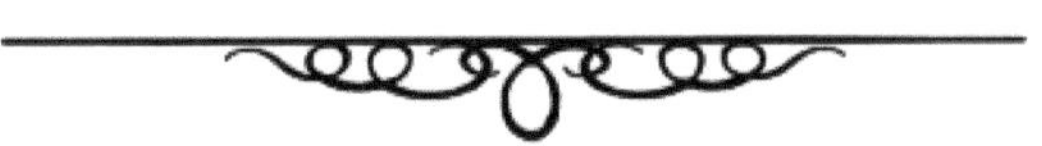

I look at the map of every day we've spent,
the careful architecture, the time well lent.
I see the foundations laid in solid trust,
the brilliant chaos settled into us.

We are a quiet storm, a chosen ground,
the one sure melody when silence drowns.
It's not just that I love you, but the way we blend.
The perfect overlap where two worlds end and a new one begins.

That easy, breathing pace,
the silent language written on your face.
I love the weight of all we've overcome,
I love us, the history that makes our spirits one.

But the world outside is sharp, the light is strange,
And sometimes fear insists upon a change.
It whispers doubts into the quiet air,
a momentary flicker of despair.

And though my heart knows the resounding truth.

Because when I weigh the future,
What I find is nothing stronger,
nothing more defined than this commitment that we built by hand.
We are the oldest story in this land.
We are the rock; the ocean cannot move.
Nothing is more durable than the love we prove.

THE SECRET SPAN

The trail was tangled, rough, and steep
Where the forest held its secrets deep
A path of roots and ancient stone
Where I walked steady and alone
But there, where the ferns grew thick and tall
Beyond the sound of the waterfall
I found a bridge, a tiny span
Untouched by any modern plan

It wasn't built for a thundering crowd
Or a world that screams its name out loud
Just weathered wood and a coat of moss
Helping the quietest souls across
A hidden link in the middle of nowhere
Suspended in the cool, green ai
Connecting the path I've already tro
To a wilder piece of the emerald sod

It didn't ask for a fee or a name
It didn't care for the city's fame
It simply waited, silver and gray
To help a wanderer find their way
And as I stepped on the creaking pine
I felt a peace that was truly min
For the most beautiful things we ever se
Are the bridges built in the middle of the tree

SOULS ALIGN

Like distant stars, a million bright,
Our love extends through endless nights.

A cosmic dance, a silent gleam,
You are my universe, my waking dream.

Across the void, our souls align,
A constellation, yours and mine.

Though space may stretch, and years may fly,
Our love, a star, will never die.

You are the stars that guide my way,
Through the darkest nights, you light my day.

A constant glow, a steady grace,
reflected in your loving face.

Like ancient stars, forever true,
My heart revolves, just for you.

A celestial fire, burning deep,
My love for you, the stars will keep.

THE DAILY CHOICE

Love is not a lightning strike, a sudden, blinding flare,
or a single, ancient promise hanging heavy in the air.
It isn't just a feeling that arrives on golden wings,
or the soft, melodic comfort that the easy weather brings.
It is a quiet morning work, a turning of the key,
the steady, intentional way that I choose to let you be.

I choose to love you when the world is chaotic and loud,
when the sun is at its zenith or hidden by a cloud.
When the warrior is weary, and the mask is full of dust,
I lean into the gravity of our unshaken trust.
It's a vote I cast at sunrise, before the day begins,
to find the place where you and I are where the story wins.

I choose you in the mundane, in the coffee and the chores,
in the way we bridge the distance between my heart and yours.
I choose you in the moments when the real is hard to face,
meeting every jagged edge with a little bit of grace.
For love is not a finish line or a trophy on the shelf,
it's the way I find a better way to give you of myself.

Every sunset, every shadow, every high and every low,
I am planting seeds of us and watching how they grow.
It's the simplest, grandest thing that I will ever do,
to wake up every single day and choose to love you.

HONEST

Like sunlight hitting morning dew,
My pride in all you do is true.
It isn't loud, but deep and vast,
A silent joy that's meant to last.

I watch the strength in how you strive,
The honest way you make things thrive.
No matter what the world may ask,
You always rise up to the task.

And though the days bring duty's call,
I promise you, you stand above all.
For every choice and every aim,
You are the constant, steady flame.

You come in first, it's always so,
The dearest truth my heart can know.
My love for you is deep and clear,
My pride, my joy, my everything, my dear.

THREADS OF GOLD

When first our paths entwined, a vibrant bloom,
We danced through days, dispelling every gloom.

Now silver threads begin to grace your hair,
And gentle lines, a testament to care.

Each wrinkle etched, a story softly told,
of laughter shared, of courage, brave and bold.

Your hand in mine, a comfort, strong and true,
With every year, my love still turns to you.

The world may change, and seasons drift and fade,
but by your side, no moment feels afraid.

For growing old with you is not a plight,
but simply loving deeper, day and night.

My dearest love, as twilight hues descend,
Our journey's beauty never seems to end.

For in your eyes, I see forever's grace,
my favorite truth, my home, my cherished place.

Always mine until the end,
your hands to hold my sweetest friend

I'LL SEE WHAT I CAN DO.

The words you spoke, a gentle, hopeful sound,
"I'll see what I can do," on love's soft ground.
Not a firm promise, bold and brightly spun,
but in that space, a tender hope begun.

For in those syllables, a kindness lies,
A willingness within your loving eyes.
A silent promise, whispered in the air,
That for my heart, you truly do care.

No grand pronouncements, no dramatic vow,
just quiet effort, starting here and now.
A gentle hand reaching across the space,
to find a way, to leave a loving trace.

Perhaps a dream I've held, a wish untold,
within your heart, a possibility will unfold.
And though the path may not be clear and bright,
Your loving effort fills my soul with light.

"I'll see what I can do," a phrase so mild,
Yet in its depths, a love for me, my child.
A gentle striving, born of sweet desire,
to lift my spirit, set my heart afire.

So let me cherish this soft, tender art.
The quiet promise held within your heart.
For in those words, so simple and so true,
I feel the strength of all your love come through.

COFFEE

The sun comes up, the coffee's made,
A silent promise, softly laid.
You speak of work, of bills, of day,
While I sit here with no more to say.
I make you laugh at something small,
But wonder if you see me at all.

You look right through me, not unkind,
To something else that's on your mind.
I long to be a sudden sight,
To stop you in the morning light.
To hear you say you see my soul,
And know that you still make me whole.

My love, I'm more than just the air
That fills the spaces you are there.
I want to feel your touch and gaze,
Like we're still in those early days.
To know that I'm not just a part,
But still the whole of your own heart.

DISAPPEARING ACT

They walk right through my silent space,
And never look me in the face.
My voice, a whisper, lost in the air,
A part of things that aren't quite there.

I sit within a crowded room,
Enveloped by a lonely gloom.
I feel the laughter, light, and sound,
But no connection can be found.

I try to shine, to make a mark,
But fade instead into the dark.
A living ghost, a fleeting shade,
A promise that was never made.

I long for just one single glance,
To feel a part of the vibrant dance.
To be seen for more than empty space,
And finally find my rightful place.

HOLLOW

An empty ache, a hollow space,
A quiet echo, out of place.

The world spins on, in vibrant hum,
but silence settles, where joy should come.

I walk through days, like painted scenes,
Unstirred by triumphs, or by sad demesnes.

A longing so deep, I can't define,
for some lost chord, or star unseen, or sign.

A shadow whispers, just beyond my sight,
A missing piece, in fading light.

I search the corners of my weary soul,
For what would make this fractured spirit whole?

Is it a touch, a word, a gentle grace?
A hidden truth, in time or space?

I reach, I strain, for what I cannot name,
A nameless longing, an unburning flame.

I'll keep going through the motions and choosing to act
Until I can feel my soul come back.

THE FACE BENEATH

I have grown so handled at the wearing of the mask,
Of answering "I'm fine" to every question people ask.
I've built a face of iron, of steady, practiced stone,
To hide the tired places that I only face alone.
I am the one who holds the line,
who mends the broken gate,
Who carries every burden and
who balances the weight.

But you have eyes that wander past
the surface of the play,
To find the quiet person who is hiding in the gray.
You see the tiny tremors in the hands
that lead the way, and the words
I leave unspoken at the closing of the day.
You look beneath the armor that I wear,
To the messy, honest human who is breathing softly there.

The miracle of being is that when the mask is gone,
when the metal hits the floorboards in the early, shaky dawn,
you do not turn your head away or ask for more disguise.
You simply love the real me with steady, open eyes.
You love the parts that feel too thin, the parts that feel too old,
the stories that are silver and the ones that are just coal.

It's a grace to be discovered, to be known and truly seen,
past the polished, busy version of the person I have been.
Behind the heavy curtain and the roles I have to play,
I am loved for who I am and that is enough for today.

THE GILDED SHARD

It is a marvel of porcelain, silver,
and light, a masterpiece worn through
the heat of the night.
Those who behold it feel suddenly tall,
They find their own strength and
they lose every fall.
When they look at the mask, they see
who they could be: Kind, courageous, and
brilliantly free. It heals every spirit and
mends every crack, giving everyone
wings while it breaks its owners back.

For the magic is fueled by a terrible cost,
By the breath of the wearer, in silence and lost.
Every smile it projects is a heist of the soul,
taking a fragment to make others whole.
It drains out the color and siphons the glow,
feeding the garden so others can grow.
While they dance in the light
that the mask provides,
the person beneath it is withering inside.

The cruelty lies in the fit of the frame,
In the way that it whispers the wearer's own name.
For though it is heavy and though it is cold,
It is the only thing keeping the heart in its fold.
The mask has become the internal design
The stitches, the glue, and the desperate line.
If she reached for the edge to let the air in,
she'd find that the porcelain is part of her skin.

It's the armor that saves her, the weight she must bear.
Holding together what's no longer there.
So she stands in the room, the most beautiful sight,
Fading to gray as she gives them the light
Bound by the magic, the gift, and the curse
Making them better, while she becomes worse.
do not mistake the fatigue for the end,
For she is a metal that's stubborn to bend.
Though the porcelain aches and the light flickers low,
There is still a fierce fire that refuses to go.
She is not a victim of the magic she gave;
She is the captain, and she is the brave.
She will march through the gray, she will carry the weight,
Until she has mastered the hand of her fate.

She's searching the world for a different glass,
Not a window for others to watch as they pass,
But a Mirror of truth, standing silver and tall,
That reflects back the person behind it all.
She will find it one night in the quiet and deep,
A place where the magic is hers now to keep.
And there, in that reflection, the healing will start,
Mending the breaks in her own weary heart
until she can stand with the mask in her hand,
Whole and unburdened, the queen of her land.

THE RUIN ON THE STREET

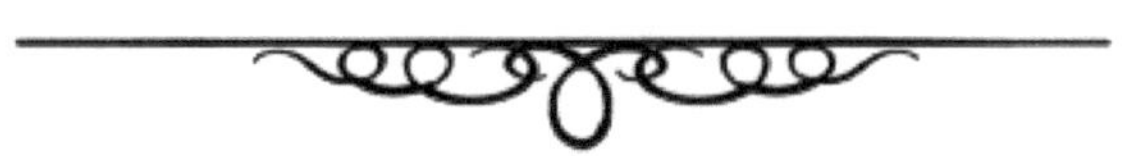

I built a town of steady walls,
Of windows bright and wide,
A place where every shadow falls
In pockets deep and hidden inside.

I carve the smiles for weary lips,
I paint the light in tired eyes,
And hold the world in steady grips
Beneath their calm and cloudless skies.

But in the center of the street,
My own house begins to bow,
The timber rots beneath my feet,
The roof is thin and weeping now.

The paint I saved for everyone
Has left my own walls gray and bare;
The work I've done is all undone
By every ghost I've harbored there.

I spend my breath to keep them warm,
To patch the cracks before they see,
While every wind and every storm
It's hollowing the heart of me.

I've built a home for every soul,
A mask for every face I meet,
But as I make the circle whole,
I am the ruin on the street.

STRANGER'S SPACE

The skin I wear is splitting at the seams,
A familiar map of who I used to be,
Now dissolving like salt into the stream
Of a life that no longer belongs to me.

The shadows stretch, the bones begin to shift,
And I am caught in the ache of the between,
Feeling the heavy, metamorphic drift
Toward a version of myself I've never seen.

It is a quiet grief to leave the shore,
To shed the safety of the old, known face,
And wonder if the person I was before
Will find a home within this stranger's space.

My edges blur, my spirit starts to bend,
An anamorphic shape, distorted and strange,
Waiting for the lonely transition to end,
Bracing for the cold, sharp wind of change.

But then I see a tired pair of eyes,
Or catch a heavy heart about to break,
And in that moment, the old darkness dies
As I choose the path only a soul can take.

To breathe a golden light into the room,
To pour my kindness into hollowed space,
Is the sun that makes the hidden garden bloom
And brings the light back to my shifting face.

In feeding them, I find my own true soul;
In lifting them, my scattered pieces mend.
The light I give is what finally makes me whole,
The grace I share is where my terrors end.

I am not lost within this new design;
I am simply growing through the dark to see

That breathing life into a world unkind,
Is how I become the best version of me.

TO BORROW YOUR MOON

The moon in my sky is a cold, silver sliver,
A lonely reflection on a dark, restless river.
My eyes are too tired, too heavy with why,
To see any grace in the arc of the sky.
They are clouded by the shadows of the days I have spent
Mending the walls where the spirit was bent.

So let me look out through the light in your eyes,
To see the same moon in a different disguise.
For yours are the eyes that still know how to gleam,
That hasn't forgotten the language of dreams.
Through you, it's a lantern, a pearl, or a ghost,
A guide for the ones who are wandering most.

I'll trade you my sadness for a moment of blue,
To see the night sky as it's filtered through you.
Where the cratered out dust isn't empty or gray,
But a playground for stars at the end of the day.
Teach me to look past the dark and the grit,
To the part of the magic that hasn't quite quit.

For when my own vision is blurred by the rain,
And the intentional life feels a little like pain,
I'll lean on your wonder, steady and true
Until I can see the whole moon, just like you.

GOLD WE GATHER AND SILVER WE KEEP

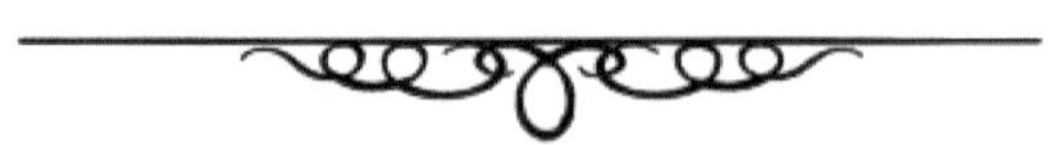

In the garden of the spirit, where the velvet shadows lie,
two different dreams are reaching for the vast and open sky.
Born of the same dark earth, under the same wide view,
but drinking in a different light to make their hearts anew.

The Sunflower is a soldier for the brightness of the day;
she finds the golden morning and chases it away.
She stands with her shoulders back and tall, a mirror of the heat,
with yellow petals burning while the world is on its feet.
She dances with the midday sun, she follows every ray,
Moving through the hours in a bright and busy way.

But the Moonflower is a secret that the heavy sunlight misses.
She waits for cooler breezes and the evening's quiet kisses.
She requires the stillness, she requires the sacred rest,
to find the hidden power that is folded in her breast.
While others close their petals up to sleep and fade from sight,
she opens like a sudden star to play within the night.

One needs the fire of the noon to stand up proud and tall,
one needs the silver of the moon to hear the darkness call.
And oh, they are both beautiful, the shadow and the sun,
the work that's done in brilliant light, the dreaming that is won.
For life is in the balance of the waking and the deep,
between the gold we gather and the silver that we keep.

ROCKS IN YOUR POCKETS

I remember the laundry, the grit, the mud and the sand,
The treasures you'd bring with a dirt smudged hand.

You'd come through the door with a grin on your face,
Like you'd conquered the world at a 5-year-old's pace.
I'd empty your pockets before the machine,
To keep all the rocks and treasures safe and clean.
A pocket full of acorns you shook from the trees.

A bottle cap shield and a tiny stick for sword,
The richest young king that the world could afford.
There were feathers and string and a marble of blue,
And I'd smile at the magic that lived inside you.
But the pockets grew deep as the boy became tall,

But part of you still wants the creek and the mud,
With the spirit of summer deep in your blood,
But part of you're reaching for things out of sight
Growing taller and stronger and chasing the light.

I want you to know, as you grow and you grit,
That the boy with the pebbles? He hasn't quite quit.
He's there when you breathe, when you lead, when you care,
In the quietest moments, I know he is there.

So keep your pockets open to wonder and doubt,
And let all that grown up and heavy stay out.

THE MIDNIGHT TRAVELER

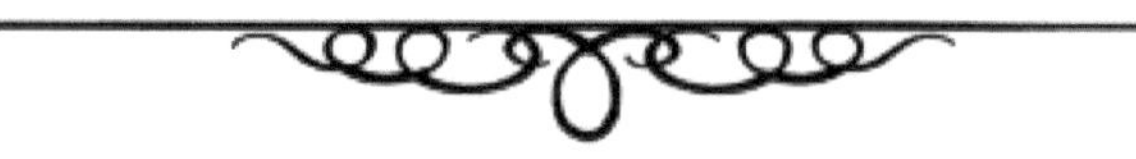

Across the roof of the frozen world,
Where the banners of northern light are furled,
A silver bell rings, sharp and clear,
A sound that only the dreaming hear.

Through the biting wind and the dusting snow,
With a velvet coat and a heart aglow,
The Master of Winter begins his flight,
To stitch together the world tonight.

He carries the weight of a thousand hopes,
Scaling the chimneys and icy slopes,
With a laugh like the rumble of distant thunder,
And eyes that hold an eternal wonder.

He isn't just a shadow, he isn't just a myth,
He's the spirit of kindness we travel with;
A bearded ghost in the fire's soft light,
Who leaves a trail of stars in the night.

He steps through the parlor with silent tread,
While the little ones sleep in a mahogany bed,
He knows every whisper, every secret desire,
Warming his hands by the dying fire.

With a wink and a nod, he's back to the sky,
Before the first morning dove can fly,
Leaving a world that is brighter and deep,
While the rest of the children are still asleep

SILVER COIN

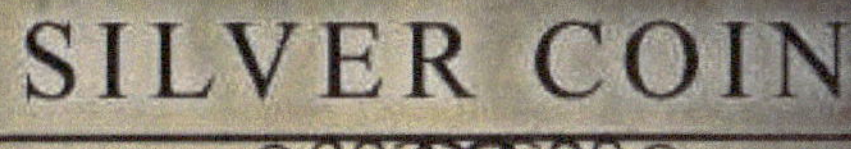

Two halves of a story, cast in the same gold,
With secrets and wonders yet to be told.
A single silver coin, tossed to the sky,
One side is the earth, and the other, the high.
Born of the same sun, but chasing the light
In ways that are different, but both of them are right.

The second is wild, with the wind in her hair,
Who finds all the magic that's hidden in air.
With eyes full of starlight and feet that must roam,
She makes every forest and meadow her home.
She dances with shadows and talks to the moon,
A whimsical heart in a perpetual tune
She is free, she is fire, she is wonder and play,
Chasing the glitter at the end of the day.

The first is still, with her roots in the deep,
With promises made and with secrets to keep.
She's down to the earth, where the clover is green,
Noticing beauty that goes mostly unseen.
She likes to sit quiet, to linger and ponder,
While her sister is out in the reaches of wonder.
She is steady and thoughtful, a calm, bracing breeze,
The wisdom that lives in the oldest of trees.

One is the mountain, and one is the stream,
One is the logic, and one is the dream.
But flip the coin over and what do you find?
The soul of a sister, uniquely entwined.
For the Wild needs the Still to find where to land,
and the Ponderer needs a bright, magical hand.
Two sides of one life, forever to be
One wild and free, one grounded and a tree.

WILD EYES AND TEA LEAVES

You carry the morning in a pair of wild eyes,
Where the sunlight is dancing and the old magic lies.
With a spirit untamed, like the wind through the pines,
you see all the beauty in the crookedest lines.
A whimsical heart that beats like a drum,
to a song only heard where the honeybees hum.

You find peace in the steam of a porcelain cup,
In the quiet of tea as the world wakes up.
With a kettle that whistles and a spoon that you stir,|
You're the keeper of secrets, of moss, and of fur.
You look for the glitter in the ordinary gray,
And turn every shadow into a new place to play.

But the wildest part of the light that you show,
Is the way that you stop to help other things grow.
With a hand held out steady and a word spoken kind,
you leave little gardens of hope far behind.
You're a healer of spirits, a teller of truth,
With the wisdom of ages and the fire of youth.

So keep your eyes wild and your heart flying free,
Between the magic you find and the pouring of tea.
For the world needs the garden that only you sow.
The girl who loves magic and helps people grow.

THE MASTER OF THE MAP

He sits at the head of a table of dreams,
Where the world isn't quite as dark as it seems.
A Dungeon Master with a heart like a hall,
Large enough, truly, to shelter us all.

He loves with a spirit that's wide and that's deep,
With secrets and stories he's honored to keep,
Guiding the party through forest and flame,
Finding the magic in every game.

He thrives on the fellowship, laughter, and wit,
Where the dice find the table and the candles are lit.
He's a hoarder of board games, of wood and of card,
A keeper of realms where the battles are hard.

But don't let the dragons or sorcery fool
The Master has one very unbreakable rule.
For all of his passion and all of his light,
He isn't a fan of the deep in the night.

He loves your company, he loves the hello
But when the clock strikes, he is ready to go.
As soon as the moon climbs a little too high,
A sleepy resolve starts to gleam in his eye.

He's a legendary hero, a friend to the core,
But he'll usher the goblins right out of the door.
For even a Master of myth and of fate
Needs his rest when the hour is getting too late.

THE SALT, THE LIME, AND THE LIFELINE

A lifetime isn't measured in the ticking of a clock,
Or the miles that we've traveled down a weary city block.
It's measured in the stories that only we two know,
and in the way we kept the fire lit when the winds began to blow.

Through the seasons of our changing, through the thick and through the thin,
There was always a familiar door that let the sunlight in.
And no matter what the world threw, or how the spirit slipped,
the foundation of our history was salt and golden chipped.

With a bowl of warm, melted queso sitting steady in the middle,
The hardest parts of living seemed a little less of a riddle.
Over margaritas glowing with lime and tart,
we'd pour out every heavy thing that weighed upon the heart.

Every late-night conversation where the moon began to fade,
every secret, every triumph, every error that we made.
We've laughed until the tears ran down and blurred the neon light,
Finding joy in being foolish in the middle of the night.

Then we've cried the tears of healing, the ones that wash you clean,
In the safety of a friendship that has seen all there is to see.
So here is to the magic in the crunch and in the pour,
that brings back every memory to the center of the floor.

For as long as there is tequila and a bowl of something blue,
there is nothing in this lifetime that I couldn't face with you.
No matter where the road goes, or how far the heart may stray,
a margarita and a reminder that 'when' will always lead the way.

THE HEART OF PURPLE

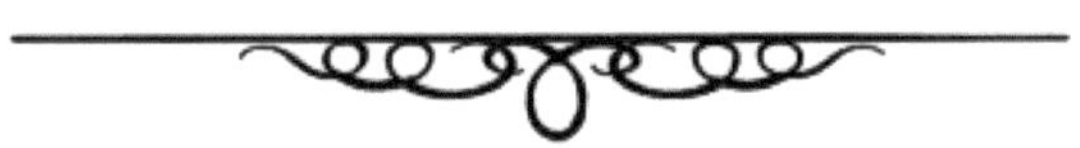

There are those who are golden, like midsummer heat,
and those who are silver, precise and discreet.
But she is the purple, the soft, rolling deep,
Where the shadows are gentle, and secrets can sleep.

She's the color of twilight when the birds find their rest,
the calmest of spirits, the kindest and best.
A welcoming soul with a violet glow,
who moves with a grace that is steady and slow.

To step through her doorway is to leave out the cold,
into a story that's purple and gold.
Her home has a heartbeat, a rhythm of its own,
The safest of places that a person has known.

It smells like the magic of cookies and spice,
Like a warm, sugary oven, a small paradise.
She wraps you in comfort and pulls up a chair,
And the weight of the world simply melts in the air.

But don't let the softness lead you astray,
For her heart is a furnace in a quiet way.
Beneath the lavender and the velvet-lined soul,
Is a ferocious love that is steady and whole.

She loves like a storm, she protects like a wall,
She's the one who will catch you before you can fall.
A heart made of purple, both tender and fierce,
with a kindness that even the darkness can't pierce.

She is the lavender, the plum, and the wine,
a person whose spirit is truly divine.
And once you have found her, you'll always stay near,
for the world is just better when Purple is here.

VIRIDIAN

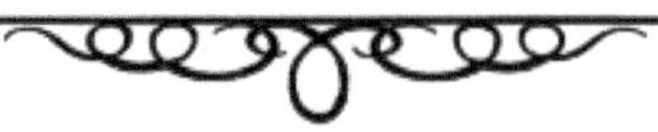

The quiet shade, where twilight keeps
A watch while all the forest sleeps,

A hue of pine and deep-set moss,
Where sunlight rarely dares to cross.

It is the Viridian, dark and deep,
Where shadows soft and silent creep.

Beneath the canopy it clings,
On ancient oaks and silent wings,

Not quite of green, not quite of blue,
But hidden, old, and solemn hue.

It wraps the trunks in velvet gloom,
A quiet, cool, and verdant room.

It is the heart of forest gloom,
A resting place, a greening tomb,

Where verdian reigns, in shades of jade,
Within the deep and tranquil shade,

A shade that rests the tired eye,
Beneath the tall trees' heavy sigh.

WHERE THE STARS SPILL OVER

The city is a hum of neon and heat,
Of pavement and sirens and crowded up streets.
It's a world made of musts and a sky full of gray,
Where the glow of the lamps steals the starlight away.
But you know a road that leads out past the glow.
Where the buildings get small and the minutes move slow.

You drive 'til the hum fades away in the glass,
Past the fences and fields and the tall, swaying grass.
Until the horizon is heavy and deep,
And the world in the rearview has fallen asleep.
Then you look through the windshield and hold your own breath,
In the quietest hollow, past the noise and the death

For there, where the shadows are honest and wide,
the stars start to spill from the dark, velvet side.
A bucket of diamonds tipped over the blue,
With a billion bright secrets all waiting for you.
No timers, no targets, no weight in your chest,
Just the sky in its glory, and a heart at its rest.

You're a small, steady light in a kingdom of sparks,
Finding the peace that only lives in the dark.
And you realize then, as the Milky Way gleams,
That you're finally out where the world starts to dream.

VELVET SKIES

As the day's long journey softly fades away,
and twilight hues in gentle slumber lay,

My thoughts, like stars that shimmer in the night,
turn only to your light.

The moon ascends, a pearl in velvet skies,
But in my heart, your brighter image lies.

Each silent breath I take, a whispered plea,
To hold you close, eternally with me.

May dreams like silken ribbons softly bind
Your precious thoughts, and peace within you find.

Let worries cease, and every shadow flee,
As sleep's sweet solace washes over thee.

The world grows still, a hush upon the land,
but in my soul, your love's a constant strand.

And as you drift towards the realms of sleep,
may your last sweet thought, my darling, I will keep.

Good night, my love, until the morning's grace,
When I can see the beauty of your face,

Sleep soundly, dear, and know across the miles,
my love for you is always wild.

WORDS TO PREACH

When shadows fall, and skies turn gray,
And whispered worries steal your day,

When paths diverge and hope feels thin,
Know that a steady hand is here within.

No judgment cast, no words to preach,
Just quiet strength, within your reach.

A listening ear, a gentle space,
To rest your heart and find your pace.

Through every storm, and every climb,
I'll stand beside you, through all time.

For in this bond, so true and deep,
A promise of support, I'll always keep.

ALCHEMY OF INK

They are only small marks on a pale, silent page,
Like birds sitting still in the wire of a cage.
But open the latch, and the magic takes flight,
Turning shadows to color and dimness to light.
With a whisper of vowels and a consonant's beat,
The world starts to shift at the soles of your feet;

For words are the architects, builders, and kings,
The invisible engines beneath all great things.
They can weave a soft blanket to cover a scar,
Or pull down the silver from some distant star.
They hold the fierce power to heal or to break,
To mend a fractured heart or to cause it to ache.

A single I love you can start a new fire,
While a cold, sharp goodbye pulls the sun from the wire.
They are potions and poisons, the balm and the blade,
the most powerful tools that a human has made.
Close your eyes and just listen: a picture appears,
of mountains and meadows and forgotten years.

They let you take flight to a faraway place,
Without ever leaving your own quiet space.
They teach you a skill, they can sharpen your mind,
leaving the dust of the ordinary behind.
They build up the bridges that help us to see
The magic that lives in what's meant to be.

So, handle them softly, or wield them with pride,
But know there is infinite power inside.
For once they are spoken, or written, or heard,
The weight of a word changes the whole world.
They make us believe in the things we can't touch,
because all these letters can mean so much.

www.ingramcontent.com/pod-product-compliance
Lightning Source LLC
LaVergne TN
LVHW021314160826
845679LV00001B/352

9798950690150